Whatsname
Street

Whatsname
Street

Anna Robinson

Smokestack Books
1 Lake Terrace, Grewelthorpe,
Ripon HG4 3BU
e-mail: info@smokestack-books.co.uk
www.smokestack-books.co.uk

ISBN 9781838198862

Smokestack Books
is represented by
Inpress Ltd

To all our dead
and all our living

Contents

What is History, Discuss?

History is and was and so is that patch
of pavement where one tiny leaf shape
is never wet no matter how much rain.
It's in the shards of clay pipes on the banks
of the Thames and the salt-glaze fragments.
It's in the loose change in my pocket
and the fact that there is never any
loose change in my pocket. It's in the bits
and bobs, the fairy on the rock cake,
at the foot of our stairs. It's t'ick
as a coddle and mild as milk.

There's a king and queen and offspring
and they're effing and blinding or not –
'cause that's common! It's in the darkness,
the rose moon, a clear deep navy sky
and a box of Price's candles to light
the longest street market in London
where we ply, plight and sing a bit.
It's in the pain of home and the urge
to command that pain with real true facts.
It is what it is, although that's contentious.
It's a bumble bee, a Brussels sprout,
and sometimes, even, a brown-tail moth.

The Back Room

How many bodies have lain in this room –
letting the sleep breath rise, coming to
with the sun, letting out groans as they shift
their legs. One, then the other. Have risen,

letting their wake breath rise, steady,
and lit a flame – lifted or switched on a kettle.
Their hands, one then the other, steady.
Found bread in a container for bread

while the lit flame burns under the kettle,
found some butter in a container for butter.
Their hands: one then the other, steady,
spreading what tastes they can bear.

It Must Start

with Dawn, as she is the only one who can no longer
tell a different story. Dawn dies,
and because we love her exactly the way we should,
her funeral is just so. There are
so many flowers, they will pull her out of the block
to the waiting hearse and the effort
needed to do this will make it seem as if she has been
here all her life – and even if they know,
no-one will choose this moment to mention that she was,
in fact, born in Battersea and came
here in the sixties, when it was all over, and we
were mostly just getting older
and not really swinging much at all.

All Our Little Chicks in a Row

Emma and Phyllis Chick – resident 1937–1939

For two years the air was still
in a changeless world. One our father
could photograph but he'd've needed
his tripod to hold steady that long.

And then, just when we thought
we'd go for it, live the life,
Uncle George, chesty and not long
for this world, came to stay.

From then on, of an evening,
after work, we'd sit together –
dinner and a chat and then
he'd settle to sleep in the backroom,

smelling of wintergreen.
We'd get out our sewing and work
on the lace for the wedding dress.
It was a summer wedding, a bit

of rain first thing but then as sunny
as you'd like, Saint John's, a party
down the pub. And then, just
before Uncle went – we were at war.

The Nightman

The Nightman comes when you most expect him to –
in your dread of him. Edgeless, shadowless, even
when lights from late-up neighbours cast rays across
the yard, and no-one you can see is there,
he creeps around the outside walls.

You can hear him collecting your dirt through
the air brick, smell him if the wind is up enough.
How the cat can sleep through this is anyone's guess.
He's piling the dirt high so it rises over
the floor line over the damp-proof course and will rise
higher yet, you'll drown in your own damp sweat,
and then he'll have what he wants – the smell of you,
warm and ripe, as it lies between you and your covers.

Filthy Filthy Woman

Boiling her beets in the copper – scooping
them out with her piss pot – then leaves it like that –
and you don't complain – she'd land
you one in the gob soon as look at you – me –
always scrubbing after her – her apron
crusted with beet juice and dribbles of lard
she'd not quite eaten – the smell of her –
you'd know she was coming before she arrived.

Shaddas

Annie, wa ya scared, them long arf li| nights?
Those dull dayz, when the fick vayls of fog drif|
tin off the rivver and claym yarrart? An yoo, payl skinned
an strong buil|, tuff enuff to face i| ead on –
wha| did you wan|? Pineapple Ada musttav known
a fing or two, Ol| Mary-Ann Ha| and Mayzie from the Nile.
Did ya know Mr Cock and Dusttol Ka|e?
Annie, they grow in roomaz in the dark, av shadda
selves tha| fetch up in the ice, singin – always singin,
az if in the back alley, on sum everlastin Sa|urday nigh|.

6 Church Walk, Lambeth (1850)

Annie Urquhart – resident 1905–1937

I come into the light in this room,
full of brown shadows and chatter.
I learnt my senses by it – our smells
contained and the sounds of outside:

church bells, cows, children, and echoes
of trains chugging in and out of the station.
On days when the sun shone, I'd be put out
to sit up in a box, or sleep, but most days

I'd stay indoors with my mother, until I grew
big enough to walk and could leave
with the others to play in the alley in front.
Daytimes, in the summer, the window was open

so we'd get an airing – even when the sky
was dark yellow, still the window was open,
and we'd hear the cows cough in their dungheap.
In my memory my mother is always scrubbing,

an old leaky bucket. Her hands red raw,
scrubbing him away – a young man
whose blue-lipped sick once whitened the stairs.

Airbricks

The airbricks sit solid – at least one I know of
in each room – iron bricks, brick bricks, with holes
that let air pass because air must do that or a space will rot.

Somewhere, under the floorboards of my back room,
something has become stale – the holes in the air brick
blocked with filth and small plastic stolen goods

and a crack where a crack shouldn't be, allowing
the smells of others to drift and hang, humming
their songs of cabbage and shit. The floorboards

are leaving the room in disgust, flaking from below
where they are hopeful of re-seeding.
When the damp man comes, all will be re-made.
When the damp man comes – please say he'll come.

Dear Sirs and Dear Lady

I trust you will pardon me taking the liberty but I feel quite justified and right in saying. I have resided here and it is my sole desire to remain. However. To my surprise – I find that my neighbours are unfair and blemished. They leave dirty things in my way and make noise that I can't even hear. This is unfair. It is unfair. I have never been a trouble to anyone. I don't like to complain.

It is the unfairness with which I consider I am rented. I make this appeal to you trusting you will give it your earnest consideration. There are bikes and skates. I come and go. I was turned down for a tenancy despite having good references. Yet, this goes on. It is clearly unfair. I trust. I put my faith in you. I apologise for occupying so much of your time. I appeal to your good judgement in these matters, which are so terribly unfair.

Miss C.

Fog, drifting in from the river, bends sound
and on days like that we hear the chimes
of Big Ben or Waterloo Station announcements
in our beds, or a voice, shouting, *That's a lie!*
across the backyards and thirty odd years.

The voice is mine and the day isn't foggy;
bright sun and our kitchen window wide open.
Miss C. is leaning over a wall that isn't there now,
telling Olive something scandalous about us;
the sound drifts up under its own steam.

As I lean out and shout, Olive ducks, runs,
wanting none of it, she's no gossip. Miss C.
hates our youth, our ease, our lack of carpet,
which is fair enough. I tell her, *I know our floors
are thin, I hear you screaming at your mother!*

That's not fair! she says, and yes, it wasn't.
I was clumsy and cack-tongued that day,
I hadn't meant she shouldn't shout at her
demented mother, I simply meant in flats
the horizon is thinner and that's just how it is.

There's something in the air that makes all sound
bend like its coming from us and one night she storms up
to find the person drilling at midnight is not us,
but in the block next door. She was kind when the cat
was ill, and soon after stopped complaining.

She told me they'd had a pub: something to do
with Charlie Chaplin. After her mother died,
the fog came for her, but there was no one
to care or yell at her; just somewhere to shove
her forehead until all her disappointments took hold.

Conditions of Tenancy 1937

1)   Rent to be paid regularly every week.

Remember when she'd come round, the ren| laydee,
         down the pub   –   on a Fryday
tagge| i| before your farvva drank i| away?

(No – no one remembers tha| – you've read tha| somewhere
and so long ago you couldn'| even say where
         i| migh|
         never 'av 'appened –
         nott'ere!)

Pay woz weekly, in yourrand, an' straight| in 'ees pocke|
         so no-wun could see
         what 'ad been deducted
         for 'is chronic lax ways

Bu| always the ren| 'ad to be pu| to one side,
         before the weekend.
         Or else the pawnshop
         or else Mrs Stubbs

2) *Tenants are responsible for seeing that the stairs, landings and passageways, forecourts and yard are kept swept and clean.*

Tha|'d be me then,   wiv the broom
        tha| leaves i|s bi|s like old
        men's 'air
        evvrywhere
so firs toff I'm sweepin their footsteps   anthen the
bleedin brissles
        anthen i| rayns
        and they all cummome
        an' I'yavvta star| all ovva aggen

3)   Tenants are responsible for sweeping of chimneys, re-glazing of
windows and any damage not caused by fair wear and tear.

There's no money tappay forra sweep
       and I ain'| going up no chimney
Your mum ain'| going up neither – can you pictur'er
       arse poking out   the upstairs neighbour's arff
       an'i|ts cold enuff
       forra wardrobe full'a waiscoa|s

4)   The street door must be kept shut.

Oh well – yes
        alright –
        and when I've lost
        me key
        and 'av
        toowask
the caretaker for the third time tha| morning... because
        no one else
        is owm in the 'ole wide world
(That would never appen   and you know i|- stop
eggsaggeratin)

Oh well – yes,
        all the flippin kids then
        in and ou|
like a 'erd of cats   an'me avin ta stop
        what I'm doin
        ta keep on le||ing
        em in

5)   No dogs, fowls, rabbits and pigeons, etc. to be kept.

You can get round this – where pigeons is concerned
      simply av no cage
      leave food forrem
      and they return,
      day in – day ou|
Like this you can have pe| pigeons, rats and squirrels
and no one   even knows   i|'s you
      But a dog,
      there's no idin one of those!

6) *No lodgers to be taken without the consent of the landlord or his agent.*

Your aunt Fanny can go to the work'ouse
   while the boys
   can sleep in shifts;
   i|'ll bee fine, i|'s always fine
We know ow ta sleep ead to toe to fit more in
We know the smell of unwashed arse in boiled wool
   when spring
    cracks
   the winda panes.

7)   No mangling or woodchopping allowed in the rooms.

Wha|, no| even when i| rains?   Ow they gonna know?
          Tha| damp'd seep
          into the walls –
          their walls –
and they ave plen|y to say if we leave the mangle in the
wash'ouse
          ee used to chop
          is wood on the landin'
they didn'| alf av words wiv us.   Much better to do i|
          indoors,
          curtains closed –
          like someone's died.

*8) No fixtures to be made in the yard or rooms without the
consent of the landlord or his agent.*

Duz tha| include our wardrobe – made by 'im
       from scraps he found,
       ou| and abou| –
       he's fixed i| to the wall
       wiv a nail or two?
       My plan| po|s from when
       I tried to make
       a little garden
on'y er from upstairs   chucked er dir| on it   ann'i| died
off?
       Duz tha| include me –
       a nigh|ly
       fixture
singin' to myself in my fron| room
       and all the sheds
       he would've buil|
       had chance
       blessed us
       with the possibili|y?

Naming the Estate

What did they (our builders) intend for us
when they left us unnamed, a small square
of streets (named for streets that went before them)
surrounded by ever larger streets and buildings –

so one day we wake up (innocent and naked)
and are so shrunk we need to know our names,
need to say them (collectively), if only to say
why we are here and in the way and what we mean

by that. (Fecktard!) At least one of us will
have to tell it with footnotes, fully referenced
(for academic veracity) in the name of a man,
born half a mile away, whose father and seven

siblings died in a plague not really worth a mention.
No wonder he loves his in text references, no wonder
I struggle to write them; shrinking as I am (a tiny
Disney house surrounded by towers) on a daily
basis (yes, daily, every blinking day).

Muvver Tongue

It came in the middle of the night – a mushroom
with so many word-spores they left a mark,
stamped him with London on his tongue.

Before that he'd spoken like a book,
called his friends *Dear Reader*, saying
to them *you pierce my soul* and *love*

seeketh not itself to please. The change
was too much for some, but for others
welcome and long, long overdue.

For most, though, it went unheard
as much of what he said was uttered
well out of range of our hearing.

'Time Has No Agreed Meaning for Historians'

Back in the day when the post came at 8.30,
I had a moment when now was all there was.
I was walking down the road when I heard
an air-raid siren and what with mutually assured
destruction being on almost everyone's lips,
that was it. It was a hot sunny day,
yet my skin was ice as if I were already dead
and we were all dead and no-one to mourn us.
And here I was, my last three minutes, spending
them clutching the railings of the recreation
ground in Ufford Street. Then came 'Ow,ow,ow'
and 'Two tribes' and I realised it was just Frankie
from a neighbour's window; and I relaxed
and slipped back into the glorious future.

Blow this forra lark!

Oo is tha| singin along Annie? Such a deep
rumbull only the pidjins can ear im righ|.
The whole world is on fiyer andjoo– so wold na,
I| urts! Annie, I listen| good and eard sum
snatches, an ee is sayin tha| for nine weeks
ee di|un| tayk is cloves off, for nine weeks
ee woz ou| wivvis shuvvull. Blow this forra lark!
ee as dreamt is dreems, as owers stitched on im
like win|ers underwear and the smell of ees body
is tarmac and big orses and enuff sawl| to floa| a navy.

Back Yard Pansies 1921

We've done our best to make a patch of garden,
even planted a vine to try to grow grapes
from seeds rescued from the bins
at the restaurant where he works as a waiter.

He wants a garden like the one back home,
but the vine died under a storm of egg shells
and cat mess. The daffodil bulbs we planted
came up but flopped through lack of depth.

That rose did well at first but bugs stripped
the leaves off it before it had a chance,
the spider plant indoors also shrank.

Nothing seems to work except these –
feral cats in purple and yellow velvet,
their faces, bold as a bunch of chorus girls.

Us, at the Seaside

1

We're all wearing It Girl hats, a ribbon
on mine and Mrs Skegg (the larger) has
a bit of a peak with a brooch fixed on.

There's a small tear in her hat but you don't
see it unless you stare and in the picture
the rent lady took you'd never know.

Mrs Skegg sits in the front on the right,
comfy in her big skirt, blouse and white
shawl and pinned on – a rose she picked
from someone's front garden as we walked.

A cross, a buckle or flower and a cardi
or not, it's hard to see what's around
the hat or the neck of Mrs Fatherly.

She is standing at the back and left
of everyone else. Although the photo
is black and white, I swear her dress

was blue with a print of flowers in yellow
or perhaps off-white. In front, a deckchair
placed just so makes her look like she's wearing
an apron – a pity, since we'd gone to such care.

...Or coat or scarf but not all three, it's spring!
'Wha| she say? – Bossy Cow! I'll wear
wha| I wan| and stand at the back of the picture,

if I so wish, wiv the oll bleedin' lo| on.
I bough| i|, paid for i|, worked bloody 'ard for i|.
Cheeky Mare! She hasta work, same as I do,

she jus'finks she gets to Lord i| over us!
Red Ha| No Drawers! She finks she's the Bleedin' Abbess!
She keeps on like tha| I'll send the boys round –
this ain't no bleedin' parade ground!'

4

We are dead and three of us wearing dresses
that are quite new, and that's the sad truth of it.
By the time you read this – hot off the press

we are dead and this is the best we can do
or maybe you've found this picture in a box
chucked in a skip after they closed the rent office.

Whatever the case, I hope you can find your way
to us, here, Whit-Monday bank holiday
sitting in deck chairs on a muddy beach,
picnics packed and stashed just out of reach.

5

With flowers, in a cotton that's not too worn,
Mrs Miller's dress covers her well as she sits
on the far left deck chair, head turned

to face the lady with the camera, an easy
smile, her bosom proud with a stolen Dahlia
or two that almost outshine her red dress.

Holding the skirt with both hands, she'll have
a paddle later, and in the fresh of that
she'll forget herself and allow a picture
with legs bare to mid-thigh, all salt licked.

We have lost our stiffness. We've been dead
to this moment, so long a winter we've had.
We had forgotten what it's like to tread

water, real sea water with sand beneath
our stiffened toes, our aching feet
with warm air round our swollen knees.

Back home again, we get on with it and forget
although some part of us is always wet
as we drag ourselves up *the garden path,*
never quite *getting the baby bathed.*

So long as tha| talk of flaars an stiffness
continues, we won'| ge| anywhere fas|
and Mrs 'owells lives by tha| – sniffin

a| the mere suggesschun of a sea|
when there's children to chase roun
the mudfla|s of Margate, by the sea.

'Er 'itched up dress has two broad stripes
ver|ical – and when she runs, i| flies
but she's never as fast as that kid ov'ers
all nobbly knees and yella curls.

8

I won't cut it! All that's left is this picture –
Mrs Stacy, Mrs Porter and three whose names
I can't remember, sunning ourselves pink

beside the sea, beside the river,
at the zoo, anywhere the coach took us,
and the rent lady'd lay on the picnic.

Our dresses are all cut from the same pattern
carefully folded back into the packet
and passed on to the next, and every rolled-up
sleeve on these dresses has the same white cuff.

9

Tiny as an afterthought, and something
sharp, like grit in your sandwich, or sand
in your bra, so when you're up and doing

back at home, and it's winter, and no-one
comes round much and you only go out
when you have to shop or run an errand,

that memory sticks and when they come
first pay day of January, we find ourselves
somehow forgetting whether it was enough
only that it was warm and we weren't so stiff.

10

Your mum said, about the feel of our skin,
that she'd sit on our knees and we were soft:
'Nanny lumps and bumps', 'Nanny two chins'.

Her children were much ruder – like little drunks
raucously singing, 'Mrs Walker ate the seaside',
and maybe she did – dive deep down and drink it.

The truth is, though our bodies were soft,
the skin on our hands was as sharp as frost
albeit red – and our feet were like sponges
dimpled and so sore we couldn't always move.

11

We are all wearing It Girl hats, a ribbon
across or a buckle or flower and a cardi
or coat or scarf but not all three, it's spring!

We are dead and three of us wearing dresses
with flowers, in a cotton that's not too worn
but has lost its stiffness. We've been dead

so long that talk of flowers and stiffness
won't cut it. All that's left is this picture –
tiny as an afterthought, and something
your mum said about the feel of our skin.

'History notoriously takes wing at dusk'

(Samuel: 1995)

Vertiginous, he says, like when, at nightfall, I fly up and out of myself and see that spot where she fell. The falling was neither the beginning nor the end of her. It was simply when we knew. There was a bleed on her brain. I don't know when it started. She was asleep sitting in her chair in the daytime when I popped round the day before, something I'd never seen her do, and it made a frail thing of her that was so much older than she would ever be.

She'd had a good morning. It was a sunny day, and she wore a new yellow top that had come from the catalogue. She went to the library (the one the council has just closed) to run a new reading group. On the way, she'd had a coffee down the market, at an outside table. I know this because at least four people seem to believe they'd had a coffee with her when in the aftermath they couldn't get their heads round it: 'but, I saw her this morning... coffee...the Marsh'.

Vertiginous, he says, and the symptoms, no wonder she fell. It isn't where she died, that spot. That was the next day, in a hospital bed, with her daughters at her side. And when she fell, it wasn't dusk, more lunchtime. But it's true. That's when it happens, dusk. I fly up, out of myself and see that leaf-shaped spot.

Thirteen at Fifteen

for the 13 15-year-olds living on the estate in 1911

Each of us is stood where we're stood
on the brink of pure fire, and sometimes we dread
what we might step off into – and always we can't wait!
Stanley Lack, Apprentice Motorworks; Thomas Ward,
Apprentice Mounter; Bill Armstrong, Press Messenger.

The end of our streets, our manor; no longer
the whole world. A night out, clean shaved, necktied,
eye-glinted, the pub or Canterbury or Ring:
Hugh Coker, Reading Boy; Victor Philpott,
Apprentice Compositor; Jim Potts, Office Boy.

And some of us not quite there yet, ever
hopeful, or with our parents' weather eye
on something 'worth waiting for...':
Benjamin Beeching, at home; Edith Welch,
school girl; Roderick Hutchinson, schoolboy.

There will never come a time when we won't be
stood in the doorway, heads turned
looking out towards the main road – saying
our names: Elsie Parker, Sweet Maker;
Wilf Threadgill, Invoice Clerk; Fred Attfield,
Apprentice Tailor; Gertie Maisie, Sweet Packer.

Infill

Between these walls the dust and bones –
the not too bad, repairs done, rent paid
on time, mostly; keep to ourselves, away
from the likes of Gray Street, happy to be south

of The Cut, still looking out for the broom
and the fitting child. Between these walls,
rubble of us, brick made of marsh-mud,
Coade stone, flint, any old muck left lying

as those streets came down. Load after load
of brick dust, cow dung that has lost its smell,
and broken glass, broken frames. It's only now
you want to hang a picture, you question the wisdom.

Block Door

Strangers, they'd come round now
and again, their backs stiff as flat irons
and their mouths! Just one straight line.
They'd look at us looking back at them,

get out their notebooks, lick their pencils
like sergeants, before their eyes flickered
to the buildings, and they'd start scribbling,
fast as their hearts beat. It was odd

the fear an unclosed door could produce
in them, I never even noticed at first,
only later, read it down the library,
how us spilling out with our fast mouths

and nitty hair, flaunting our dirt
on the public highway could herald
the end of everything. Not to mention
the children, organised and armed

against each other with sticks
and binlids, and constant shouts
and the babies – all smiles and spit,
just lazing around in boxes.

Miss Sunderland

'Ladies must do it, for it is detailed work; ladies must do it, for it is household work; it needs, moreover, persistent patience, gentleness, hope...'

Octavia Hill

She ran the 'ole thing – she run the 'ole estates. I remember when I was a school kid, they used to do the 'ole ou|side every two or three years. Coz her family were builders, so she knew what should be done. When the people come – the pain|ers and tha| – they had 3 tier ladders – coz they never had whatsanames – scaffolding then. They used to pu| the ladders up and work across. They'd done the whole side and she came around and the bloke in charge – the foreman – he said, 'I|'s all done now, Madam, shall we take the ladder down?' and she said, 'No, leave i|' and she climbed all the bleedin way up to the top and she stood ou| on one of those... she stood right up the top, looked down into the gutters and she turn round on the ladder and said to the foreman, 'Soandso – would you like to come up here?' I mean right up at the top, as large as life and he turned round and his face went ... he wen| up there and she said, 'You haven'| finished this'; she said, 'You're paid to pain| the gutters'; she said, 'You've coa|ed i|, but you haven'| cleaned the dirt out.' She took a knife, and she scooped the dirt out – they'd lef| the dirt in – they hadn't cleaned it off, and do you know what she did – she stood on the top of one of those and she put a mirror beyind the standpipes and she said they adn'| done those, so she made them do i| all again before she would pay 'em.

*

Her pebble glasses, bottom of bottles,
her face round to match, her coat – black
as her tenants' coats, her hat – their Sunday
best, dress – floral, stockings – thick
and serviceable, shoes – black with small heel,
laced. Undergarments – fully controlled.
She's up that ladder, no nonsense broached,
checking for dirt, for slacking by men
who were born tired and died that way.

An Utterance

to Utter:
To pass forged coins into the money system by spending it

Not a rag to wipe the snot off a child's face,
and so when he comes with his snowfall
of silver and bronze – I think 'yes!' and
'tonight we'll eat' and all I have to do
is spend them and pass him the change.

When you dig down through all the mud slung,
you'll see the one I hid for you, child,
untattered by testing, unuttered, so shiny –
your's'll be the face on it, so shiny
it gave me away, the farthing I kept for you.

Street Party 1935

Recreation Ground, Ufford Street/Mitre Road

A moon on her hat, a feather on his, mock nippies tied together with one ribbon, a flower bigger than the wearer's head, a couple of paper crowns, a pointy, jester, pirate hat, three round-head tin hats – little soldiers, all cut up with bunting.

Big bowls of stuff to serve into smaller bowls, and plates of triangular sandwiches, plates with sausage rolls, a slice of ham, slab cake and cups of tea with milk and sugar and it's all for the kiddies – only for the kiddies, and all sliced by bunting.

The ladies, in pinafores with waitress hats but no buttons, overblown bosoms and cardigans ablaze. Her heavy coats. Her outmoded hats. Her busy busy. Her standing with the girls. Watching the kiddies and all those slices of bunting.

More men than you notice at first – suited and watching – from the back. Except him, with both hands on the teapot, must be enamel, must be red, playing mum. Him with an accordion and beret. Him with a megaphone in his hand. All cut up with bunting.

And you, who said you could stand on the seat, eat that yet, cry, stare up at the sun, wander off with your thumb in your mouth – and you, who said you could look creased by sleep walking into the wind, who said you could take your hat off, who said you could get cut up by bunting?

Terry's Haibun

My mother was small then; they lived in The Cut. You wouldn't remember Mark Antonio's, the ice-cream place. On the corner you had the co-op. Where the launderette used to be – was Mark Antonio's. My gran used to live out the back in what they used to call The Lids. It was all low – the shops was underneath and they was all above. The same as these but bigger rooms. Of course, there was no electricity, it was gas then. The people that used to own where my gran lived was people named Geest and they used to have to go and pay the rent down on the Westminster Bridge Road. Where the bank is now, they had a rent office. Of course, you had, the wasaname in the corner – back end of the Cut, there used to be a pawn shop on the corner there.

My mother and her sisters; my grandfather worked on the docks – down the Surrey Docks. He used to walk down there and if he was lucky, if he wasn't back by 8 o'clock, he'd got work. My gran used to send my mother or her sister down the docks and if he'd got work, he'd give my mother or her sister a couple of bob so they could come home and get some breakfast.

> Long walks
> bruised pears
> for breakfast

My mum lived on The Cut, lived over the wasname, they had 3 bedrooms. My mother and her sisters all slept in the one bed. They had the old stoves. You could cook your Sunday dinner in there and they had the old swing hobs. The old fixed light company were the first electricity we had, you couldn't plug in an iron or a radio. My uncle was an electrician so what he did – he built a little transformer so my mum could have an iron. He used to take the lightbulb out and clip the iron in. It was dodgy.

My mother was saying – she said – these used to be back to back and one day a load of horse and carts and 200 Irish navvies appeared and it was all by hand, no drills, all pick and shovels, dug up all by hand – loads of stones dug out by hand. All the rubble was all tossed in four carts, all pulled away by horses.

The Windmill
or Buttercup
a frontier at noon

My mum would go out shopping on a Saturday morning, when I was small, I'd be in a pram. I mean she would leave the door open, or wouldn't lock it and she'd leave bread and cheese on the table – milk, sugar, kettle'd be sizzling on the hob, she'd leave the money – you wouldn't dare! Now you'd lock your door to go out in the yard – in those days you could leave it wide open – no one would take anything. Co-op Milkman, the Baker used to come in – there was an old baker, we used to call him Rustus, he had an old cart, a two wheeled cart. He was a funny... his talk ... he had a stutter, don't know why he was called that – Rustus! He had this cart and it was quite heavy and he used to haul it and he used to deliver the bread. The milkman never had a van in those days, it was horse and cart, and he'd load up a couple of bottles of milk or whatever he had to deliver and he'd go and deliver what he had then he'd come out and whistle and the horse'd come along. My mum always left him some bread and cheese or something or a sandwich or something and he'd eat it, that's probably his dinner cause he'd be out about 5 o'clock in the morning, especially on a Saturday or something, cause he had to go and collect his money, he probably wouldn't be home till about twelve o'clock at night.

Oh – yes! Because he'd have to go round and collect his money and if he got back to the depot, where he'd have to put his book and his money in, if he hadn't got enough he'd have to put it in. If someone couldn't pay, he'd have to put it in himself – otherwise he'd 've got the sack. There was nothing else – there was three million unemployed.

> Horse whistling
> down long days –
> taking the biscuit

Don't forget the Church Commissioners: if you couldn't pay the rent, out on the street you went. It was only the workhouse then, that's all you had. If you had a spare shirt you were lucky, if you had a spare pair of trousers... I mean, you went to school and you had a hole in your shoes, you put a lump of cardboard in them.

I remember my mum saying, there was 4 of them, I remember her saying if it was wet and we'd only got one pair of shoes, she'd carry her on her back to school so she wouldn't get her feet wet. In those days, if you had the doctor, you'd have had to pay a shilling. Not like nowadays. People don't realise it – there's not many left now, but apart from anything else...

> Gloria Swanson
> loved my silver shoes
> holes an' all

I've lived on this estate, we moved up when I was three, so for 83 years. We lived in Crozier Street before, near to St Thomas's hospital. My dad, before he went to work, he had to go downstairs and bring up 3 or 4 buckets of water coz you never had any water, you had to go down the yard and get it, you had a tap in the yard, my dad used to bring it up.

I remember, one day my mum had to go down the yard and get a bucket of water. It was heavy, they were heavy and (remember those big old buckets, those cast iron buckets) one of those and she spilt some water on the stairs and was going to clean it up and this bloke – the bloke what owned it – miserable so and so, he really got nasty over it and one thing led to another and he shoved my mother over. I think he pushed her or something. My father come home. Oo, he went down and he... That's how we moved down here. He opened the door and my dad's gone wallop! And I mean, my dad wasn't small, my dad was as strong as bleedin 'orse, I mean my dad was strong. I've seen my dad lift 400lb off the floor over his head. He hit this bloke once and then we moved. He left a week's rent on the table and this bloke was just about coming round and he said we're leaving and we went round to my gran's, and my aunt, one of my mum's sister's, had just got a place down here. That's how we got a place here.

> Water flows east
> follow
> the trail home

It used to be 52. Not the block next door, the one after. We had two rooms on the ground floor. Where your sister lives. It used to be 52. It was the only block that got fire bombed and so it's different now, but that is where we come to. It was a two room. One large front room and a box room. When I got bigger we moved to a three room flat. For two rooms, the rent was, I think, half a crown, course half a crown was a lot of money. You could get a leg of lamb for sixpence.

Do you want a cup of tea or something?

*

The best night I ever had was at The Scala, Milan. It was an opening performance of La Boheme. And er – Maria Callas and Guisepe Di Stefano – it was a gala night. So, we went in dress uniform. Dave and his wife, she was Italian, and I was courting an Italian girl at the time, Francesca, and we got a box. Our dress uniform was blue jacket, dark blue trousers with a scarlet stripe down, glengarry, and of course, we were both Sergeant Majors so we had epaulettes over the top, the girls both had nice evening dresses on. It was a beautiful night, some gorgeous music.

I went in the army in 47 and spent five years in, National Service. I got promoted, got made sergeant. I remember the old man from our company, he said 'You're a sergeant now' he said 'If you stay on you could'... cos my time was nearly up, he said 'If you signed on for three more years you could get as far as RSA even more'. So, I did a short service agreement, that was for another 3 years. Then I come out.

> Long road south
> and north again
> brown-tailed moths

There used to be some rough hard core families down here. There was one this side of the rec., Bowers their name was. There was a father and mother but the old woman used to rule the roost. Poor old man, but she was a very large woman, you know, and her husband was quite an easy going man. And she had a son and two daughters and the son, he was one of those big tall skinny blokes with long gangly legs, know what I mean. If he was out somewhere and he wasn't in, she used to go out to the door and if he hadn't come in and she used to shout 'Sonny!' she used to shout – you could've heard her down the Blackfriars Road.

But he turned out, they all turned out – she had two daughters, they turned out! I think the oldest girl married well off, the other girl, don't know what happened to her, but he did alright – Sonny. He was one of these who always had his head in a book, studious, he finished up.... He went in the army and finished up a Major. He was a very clever lad.

> Sonny and me
> heads in books
> and staying there

There used to be a doctor's surgery on the corner of Blackfriars Road donkey's years ago. He was an Irish doctor that used to be in there. He was really, really a real broad Irish man. When I was a kid you used to have to have money. The only chance, if you ever got to a hospital, you had to be really ill, on death's door virtually. Anything you didn't know, you relied on your gran.

My gran knew more than anyone else. You'd go round your gran's or get your gran round. Things like that. My gran knew about herbs and that. My mother's parents. My mother's father – he was Irish. Course – I got a bit of both – I'm half Irish, half Welsh. But – em – gran knew everything. I can remember having, I think I must have been about four or three and a half, I think. I caught pneumonia... my gran... you couldn't get a doctor if you didn't have the money. My gran used to get stuff from down the Walworth Road, used to go to Baldwin's and get Russian Tallow, and it was... smelt like camphor... used to get this flannel and heat this Russian Tallow till it was really very hot and when I was ill, I was very cold and she got it hot and smacked it on me, here! And it would either kill or cure. If it was too hot it'd burn you! She used to bung this on and she said to my mother you have to get this on three or four times through the night – and it cleared it out.

This Irish doctor, if you went to him, Lanagan his name was. He was rough and ready, used to swear, effing and blinding, but he was a good doctor. I 'member, my mum's sister was ill one day. She wasn't very well. Lanagan come out, big bloke he was, well! and he liked a drink, well he used to drink with my grandfather. My grandfather came from Cork and he knew old Lanagan, he come from the same place and he used to drink like a horse, drink like a fish. He come round, my grandfather got him to come and see my mum's sister and of course, he saw all the windows closed, all the curtains drawn and anything to stop the draft coming in and Lanagan walked in and he said, 'God almighty woman, you'll bloody kill her get the bloody windows open, you're killing the girl'. He said, 'Have you got any beer in the house,' and she said, 'Yeah'. He said, 'Right', he got a bleedin great jug – he put three or four bottles of stout in a saucepan and boiled it up till it got hot, got three eggs put it in, stirred it round and said – 'Get that down ya!' He would always be giving the kids Guinness – saying 'Get that down ya!'

But, I mean when I worked in Smithfield Market, the porters, they would still go down the pub and they would get... for breakfast they'd get a couple of quarts of Guinness, put three bloody eggs in it and a hot poker would go in there, yeah! Get a hot poker and stick it in the jug. That was the best breakfast in the world in the middle of winter.

> The horse man
> brings air,
> herbs and beer

There was another family down there, the Webbs. And his wife was quite a lady for round here, quite tall, would never go out without gloves, always wore gloves and court shoes. The father, he was a seaman, he was in the merchant navy, and in the war he got torpedoed twice. I 'member when he come home, when he come home, he was on a boat for god knows how many days. He come home and they'd throw him any clothes they could find. He come home and he had an old pair of trousers on and an old shirt and it was bloody cold. I remember he come in and his wife was practically in tears. I remember when my mother saw him and she said, 'Good God – he looked absolutely dreadful'. Well, I mean, being in the bloody Atlantic in the middle of winter and being torpedoed in an open boat for about 28 days, how would you feel! Well, he went back again and twice he got torpedoed. But he kept at it and when the war was over he retired and they moved away somewhere. I got an idea that she was, I mean she was always pleading poverty but she was shrewd and I think she put a bit of money away. I think they went to Hampshire or somewhere. I think she bought a house down there, a cottage or something.

> Cold cold water
> one eye on the task
> the other on home

My gran had two cats and there was a woman a couple of doors away, she had a fish stall and course she used to cut up all the fish on the table to take down for the fish stall and it was a warm day on this particular day and so she had the door on a-jar. Course, one of the cats we had, he was always on the look out for anything and one day he butted in the door and got in there and she had a plate with all cod fillets on the table. The two of them went in there and scoffed the lot didn't they. She come out and just left the plate there with the fish. Course my gran was doing the laundry and I was helping her. I was turning the handle of the mangle for her. She came running out, she had a mouth on her this woman did. She picked on my gran, she picked on the wrong one. My gran wasn't small. A big woman my gran was. And she said, my gran said, 'Well it's your bleedin' fault you silly cow! Leaving the bleedin' door open in the first place,' she said. I mean, this woman went in pretty quick and shut the door, she'd a got the back of my gran's hand, she'd a gone down quick. But, afterwards when she calmed down and it all calmed down, the woman come out, and she – my gran – could see... she could see... she said 'Ma', she said 'Mari, I tell you what, I'll pay for the bloody fish' and course after that, that was it! That was how they used to do things. If she'd have come any closer, my gran would have floored her.

> Floored fish
> sorted the
> cat's whiskers

If you've got an empty place next to you, new people moving in, my mum used to put the kettle on for them. I remember when we lived in 52, we lived at the top and there was a couple there. The boy was roughly my age, Ronnie. Ash their name was. His wife was talking to my mum and her husband was only a little tiny man and living at the top... they had a horse and cart with all their... you remember those great big old double beds, your gran had something like it when she was young, and course this bloke had no hope in hell of getting this up the stairs and the old bloke, who had the horse and cart, said 'No mate, I don't touch any of that,' he said, 'I just drive the 'orse and cart, I can't help you. I'm not going up there with that bleedin' lot', so course my dad had to help him, I said, 'He'll never lift that off there, it'll kill him' and my dad said 'Oh well, alright, I'll go and give him a hand.' He rolled his sleeves up and went down stairs and said,

'You in trouble here, mate?' and he said, 'Yes – I can't even lift it off the cart. I don't know how I'm going to get it up the stairs', so my dad picked it up and ran up the stairs with this great big bed and said, 'Where d'you want this, love?' and put it against the wall. Anything heavy, my dad took it upstairs for them. This bloke, I think he was a clerk in an office or something. Most of the men who lived down here were either dockers or printers or worked in a foundry or something. Not clerks. Most men were labourers and were strong.

More clerks than you'd think
Terry, love!
Deep in the paperwork

The Mother in Law's Nets

In the shadows and whoops of the last of the party
she slipped back indoors and took down the curtains,
      brown with war and the filth of outside.

In the dim flicker of the hallway light, she filled
the sink with water and soap and dipped each
      like it was made of the very best lace

and with each rinse her tears salted the water.
They fell silently at first but as the dirt ran out
      and down the drain she could be heard,

by the neighbours, gently sobbing, and by the time
the nets were white again, howling, fit to burst,
      you could even say she had.

Nostalgia

Maureen Robinson – in residence 1986–2007

There's an old bear, lacking eyes and an arm.
There's a hole in his face and much of his fabric
is worn bald and thin, and yes, he's not a real
flesh and blood bear and hence, not 'he' as such.

I've not brought him with me because I'm no
longer a child. *Nostos* means a return
home, and mine will be by train, a forward-
facing window seat with a fold-down table.

Throughout the journey, I will look at
pictures on my phone of trips made this year,
of family and pets. I will listen to music
and at the half-way point eat a sandwich.

Then I'll take a short bus ride through
a central London evening; there'll be a light
mist of rain that fogs the windows, and I'll
make one 'I'm on the bus' call to my sister

then sit back as we circle The Aldwych.
Crossing the Thames means *nostos* even
though our mother is dead. The lights
slash the water and ripple; the beach is quiet.

In Waterloo, I'll get off the bus and drag
my suitcase, go home to where the bear
is sitting in the bedroom, with one more month
of dust on him. There's pain from being away

and pain for what is lost and, some say, pain
for what was never there, but she
were there, of that I'm sure; we are still
her daughters, even though she's dead.

The Crimes of Mrs Williamson

She spi| on my 'ouse flannel, spa| on my vegtibbles: block| the copper flu with payper: greased the WC pan when it was 'er turn to clean. The WC 'as two mops beyind the door. a grea| lump ov motor tyre on the door. boxes ov wood. so we canno| empty our bucke|s. the mats are shook on the landin and they chop wood on the landin, early mornin, the dir| swept under 'er neybuz door.

She stamps 'ard, throws 'eavy articles abaat the room. early mornin' racin' up and daan, slammin' the doors and making a row: when asked to keep quie|, shouts owt: 'gettinsyd you dirty forinner' then spa| in our face – said they 'ad been waiting for this. Insul|ed us. by saying I was on'y a chorus girl on'y earning free paand. She doesn'| 'ave to earn 'er living: but when at 28, she worked on munitions. She lef' at 5.30 and made enough noyz to wake everywunup. told several peepull in the street she bought flaas for Miss Way when she was ill when she nevver went near tha| fla|. Told the old laydee she wan|ed a penny ra||le and she woz on'y 'ere to keep the passage clean.

I'm an old cunt

I know this because a man
once shouted it from the rooftop

to my mother, and I didn't fall far
from that tree. He was fetter and addle

and not long off being sacked both
by the boss and any cunt given with love

by any cu – be she cow or queen.
Cu is skin and soft; she is a hidden

shelter, a river running underground,
a Nordic wife. She remembers Mary Allcunt

and Cuntha Cronch and poor Fanny, alone
in Hastings with three children still at home

and all of us who never took flight
from any eggshell, and if it's true that y

is simply an x with a missing leg, then
we're all cunts, all born from cunts.

Binless

Leaving[i]- no[ii]- footprints[iii]-, he[iv]- passes[v]- through[vi] -
From[vii]- above[viii]-, no[ix]- history[x]-, no[xi]- need[xii]- of[xiii]- a[xiv] bin[xv]-.
He[xvi]- was[xvii] - here[xviii]- and[xix]- spoke[xx]- to[xxi]- one[xxii]- of[xxiii]-
    us[xxiv]- once[xxv],
Now[xxvi]- he[xxvii]- is[xxviii]- gone[xxix]-, and[xxx]- the[xxxi]- clean-up[xxxii]-
    team[xxxiii]-
Making[xxxiv]- more[xxxv]- noise[xxxvi]- than[xxxvii]- he[xxxviii]- ever[xxxix]-
    made[xl]-
On[xli]- all[xlii]- the[xliii]- days[xliv]- he[xlv]- lived[xlvi]- there[xlvii]-.

Back-Yard Megalith Stone Thing

The thing, installed in the sixties, made of stone,
was born with an old spirit, perhaps Coade stone.

A simplified Eleanor Cross marking our space.
We hung one end of our washing lines to this stone.

The other end was hung to a fixed plate on the wall
secured by flat-headed screws sunk in stone.

In the plate's centre, a ring strong enough
to take a hanging basket weighing at least a stone.

Back then, just one line, with sheets, a dress
and maybe underwear the colour of stone.

The thing, once seen or imagined, cannot die –
even when you saw it with your own eyes – stone

smashed to its core, then carted off
in barrows to a skip full of fractured stone.

Not even then can I not feel its central pull
and try to locate myself by this sense of stone.

Agadoo

Loosely speaking a circle of us, our arms
are thinking 'trees' and bend stiffly
on the right word. It's been a while,
we aren't sure of the first move and laugh

with what-am-I-like-eyes, then we are off,
second nature, pushing pineapples, grinding
coffee. Roughly speaking or loosely – according
to mood – we are to the left, to the right,

with a mid-point not-sure shrug. We jump,
not 'up and down' but slight, on our toes, quick
so's to be ready to touch our knees. Remember
when we could do all this and sing along
thinking for god sake, don't let anyone see!

Ta||ered

The ta||ered cur|ains in the doorway, layers of dust up the
     passidge,
ow|to the frun| door, streeked in greess, and the step has no|
     bin cleend
in years. I dred to fink wo| er stowv looks lyke! Wha|duz she
     doo all day?
She's no| a drinker, I don'|fink she's doo-lally, she olds down
tha| job ovvers. Mrs Albrigh| wen| in wun day to warsk if she
     wan|ed
in for the Chrissmuss club and sed, she woz si||in by the fiyer-
     plays jus| starin,
as if in a trarnss, no| a| the flayms bu| the spayss abuv, the
     soo|y bi|.

The wind woz roarrin in the chimnee, an Mrs Albrigh| woz
     wunderin
if tha|'s wha| she woz wurreed abow|, the wind, althow no|
     wurreed exac|ly,
she di|en| look wurreed, she di|en| look nuffink! Mrs Albrigh|
     sed she coul|en|
pu|er finga on i|, jus| tha| she seemed lyke she wasn'| there.
She spowk to er and nevver go| a reply, so she took the ump,
sayin *That is a rood, ignorran| woman and she can sor|erself
     ow|!*
She duzzen| cum ow| on the doorstep, she duzzen| go down
     the pub,
nor is she wun fa the church. Just off to work and back,
as if she's nevver lef|, an all the time, starin a| tha| wun dark
     spayss.

One Day

it was quiet except for the small hum
of life and chat from the market and the odd
fight spilling out of the pub and then
one day, round the corner they came, stepping
out of dust clouds, navvies with their horses
and carts. Every lunch time they'd stop – a split
second of deafness before the crunch of feet
heading for the pub and even though they could
have filled them all: Anchor and Hope, Coach
and Horses, Jolly Miller, Pear Tree, and some,
they just crammed in to The Windmill. A pint for each
and a large tray of bread and cheese with pickles
and twenty minutes later, when the whistle went –
they'd be out of there, or else the boot.

Some Nights

Sometimes it seems that all night long someone who treads heavy, perhaps a big boned man, walks up and down the corridor upstairs. What is he looking for? My ear reaches out to the ceiling saying, settle big man, there is nothing in your cellar other than a woman with out of control hair who, more often than not, overthinks things.

Some shadows are longer than others. If I move that glass, the water will shimmer with moonlight, and that would be wrong. If I move the clock, its red light will scatter across the flat of the wall and disturb its smooth line, and I would see the time in reverse, which would be not quite as wrong. If I move my self, the water of me will shift and settle and my dreams stir.

Early May Bank Holiday

The back yards hum with our heat as we lean into
our summer chairs with whatever we are treating
ourselves to close at hand; content to be shiftless.

The windows are open and the music of summer sings
out from high toilet windows in whistles. On one side
of a low wooden fence, two households have sited

ourselves either side of a path of plant pots.
We call to each other with jokes read from phones.
Over the fence a barbecue wafts, and we drift in

and out with food, more drinks, a magazine. Over the fence
the radio's on and later Bowie, very loud, and we smile,
sing along, before the cool falls and we gather our bits and head in.

Then later, getting the cat in – didn't you hear their granny
singing 'a chair is still a chair' and then later, letting it
out again, in the pitch black, didn't you hear the clatter

of them tidying up, then the light from their shed flooding
out and their granny's voice, loud and proud, taking
her spotlight 'tonight Matthew, I'm going to be...'

Acknowledgements

Thanks are due to the editors where these poems or earlier versions were first published: *Compass, Brittle Star, Poetry Birmingham, Cake, Oxford Poetry, Long Poem Magazine, 1110.*

I would also like to thank the Archivist and staff of the following archives and libraries: Church of England Archive, Lambeth Archives, Southwark Archives, London Metropolitan Archives, British Library, National Archives, Guildhall Library, Museum of London Archives.

My thanks also go to my colleagues in the Creative Writing Department at the University of East London and especially to Kate Hodgkin, who supervised the thinking behind this project for my PhD, and to Mary Chamberlain and Carrie Etter for their helpful comments.

My thanks also go to Terry Jones, Doreen Gilbert and her daughters Lisha and Tracey, Doreen Day, the Bowds, and my own family – and many other neighbours – for their stories and for helping me make my stories.

Notes

Filthy Filthy Woman
This poem is taken from oral history collected by Mary Chamberlain and published in *Growing Up in Lambeth* (Virago, 1989).

'History notoriously takes wing at dusk'
The title of this poem is taken from an editorial by Raph Samuel in *History Workshop Journal*, Autumn 1995

'Time Has No Agreed Meaning for Historians'
The first 12-inch (annihilation) mix of *Two Tribes* by Frankie Goes to Hollywood, (1984, ZTT records) featured an air-raid siren. My best guess is that this was being played from Angie's window.

The Crimes of Mrs Williamson
The original letter complaining about Mrs Williamson's behaviour disintegrates into a very odd syntax that includes some rather random fullstops. I have kept that in this poem, even though it is a translation into voice.

Binless
i   This leaving is infinite
ii   and as well as infinite it does not exist
iii   in so much as there are no footprints, no prints visible of his feet, on the stairs, in the hallway or by the bins, taking into account that it snowed at least twice during the time he lived here. Plus he has never actually been seen in the backyard, apart from briefly on the last day of his tenancy. Strange.
iv   He is a young man with sandy hair, who regularly received postcards from his mother from Jersey – although sometimes they were bought in London from art galleries, just postmarked Jersey.
v   This leaving is infinite if not always expressed that way,

vi   through all the corridors of his 5 room flat and the shared stairs, hallway and yard.

vii   We thought he might be from Jersey, but from his mother for sure, she being his only visitor, apart from that one time, a dark haired woman who wound up with a parking ticket.

viii   The top floor tenant is always apart in the block. There was the elderly woman before him, who woke the whole block one night at 3am with a Barry Manilow Karaoke. Before her, a gap in my memory, and then years back, a woman and her aging daughter, slow as violets in a very small vase.

ix   Whatever follows is not

x   what we are built on and how we define it and the way we tell that to ourselves and others

xi   Whatever follows is not

xii   a sense or feeling that creeps mostly through the gut and upwards, although it can effect the legs, resulting in panic if unfulfilled.

xiii   The part and the whole and its relationship

xiv   and this – the first letter, and the first letter of my name, and the address of the man who shouts Bitch! at me when I prune the yard rose.

xv   The young man was a quiet man, so quiet he was forgotten by the council and the estate managers, when the bins were given out and never had one. But he never made much rubbish and didn't mind. Did they ever wonder where his rent money appeared from?

xvi   The young man, sandy hair, whose mother lives in Jersey,

xvii   had been

xviii   in Webber Street, just south of the river

xix   and – isn't there always some kind of connection between one thing and another

xx   his voice was quiet but clear and whilst not unfriendly, did not invite conversation, he told me his television wasn't working either, when I asked the night the block's aerial was blown off-course, otherwise, when we met in the hallway, he would nod 'hello'

<table>
<tr><td>xxi</td><td>and this nod was addressed towards a point or person, always</td></tr>
</table>

xxi   and this nod was addressed towards a point or person, always

xxii   a singular action, pure and intended

xxiii   regarding its relationship to the part and the whole

xxiv   We – that is me, the shouty man, the family in between, and Doreen G., who has never seen him in the backyard only out the front, being the whole – he the part.

xxv   He only spoke to me that once, on the landing, about the television.

xxvi   At the precise point you read it, dear reader,

xxvii   that young man with sandy hair, whose mother lives in Jersey

xxviii   is to be

xxix   no longer here on our estate, and therefore now of questionable existence as he only lived here 3 years or so

xxx   and, yes, there is always some kind of connection between one thing or another

xxxi   the actual – almost Godlike thing– and we – me and the shouty man and the family between – have no power over it at all. However many letters we may write.

xxxii   They come every time someone moves out now, paint, change over fitted kitchens and whatever else, but only to the market rent flats and they bang and bang and bang. They are banging while I write this and when you read it, they are still banging – but probably in a different flat by now.

xxxiii   They (those that say this) say there is no I in team, but there are lots of other letters that are also not in team, such as Z or J.

xxiv   They make good by dint of the sweat of their brow and the 'sorry love' of their lips

xxxv   everyday since the young man left they have come and come again and banged and drilled

xxxvi   the dull thud of their hammers and the white high wiz of their drills has become music to me

xxxvii   and now I will compare this to something else

xxxviii   to him, the young sandy haired man and his mother, who visited occasionally, to a long, long word – ever – predating us all, even the brown-tailed moths that infest the street trees every 50 years or so, even Lacteria, who will not accommodate the disorderly, even the first purpose built circus that pissed off William Blake and it's a word that stretches on into the future, and its colour is Gold or Grey depending on your mood. And – he has his blink and you'll miss it moment

xl   by dint of the sweat of his brow, the young man with sandy hair and a hello nod

xli   supported by or balanced on top of

xlii   the total number of days that he lived here

xliii   the actual definite number

xliv   of units of 24 hours, and despite that some are definitely longer than others, and some days you can go without seeing anyone, just hearing them, and that sound is as sweet as bird song on a short winter's day

xlv   Young man, sandy hair,

xlvi   the conditions for life are air, water and food, and so we must assume all these were present in the upstairs flat. Doreen said she saw him out of her front window, carrying his food back from the shop with no bag, just his little microwave dinner in its packaging.

xlvii   To this place, our estate, Whatsname Street.

Ta‖ered

‖ is a punctuation mark that I created to use as a London glottal stop. Traditionally either a space has been left or an apostrophe used, but this stands for an absence and that isn't right. The London GS is an identifiable (if subtle) sound. Punctuation marks from other languages that use GSs – such as the Hawaiian Okina or the Arabic Hamza – were not quite right either – because they represent much more stressed, back of the throat GSs. I chose this symbol ‖ because it is part of an internet language range of GSs and because it is reminiscent of an Aliph – which often goes with a Hamza in an Arabic GS – so it had some links to established symbols for GS. But, its slimness and length carries a suggestion of subtlety – an image of stopping slightly and has a trace of t-ness in it.